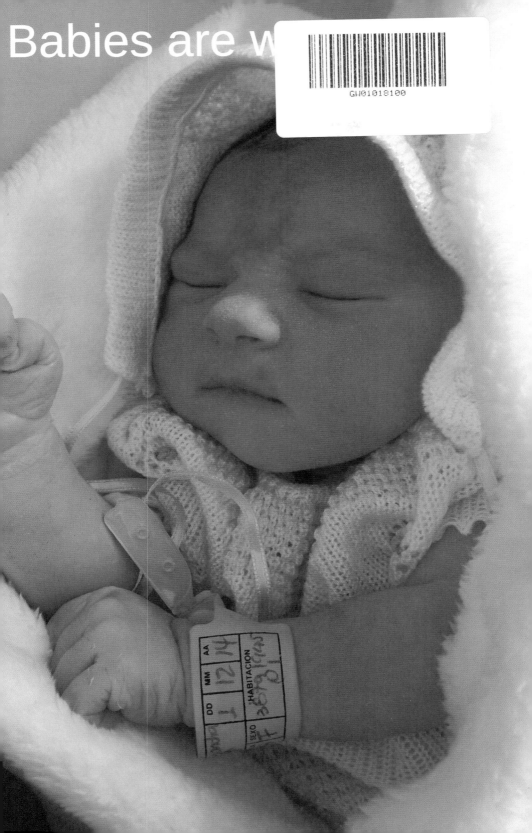

Babies are w

GW01018100

Babies love to smile.

All is well.

I am contented.

The World is amazing

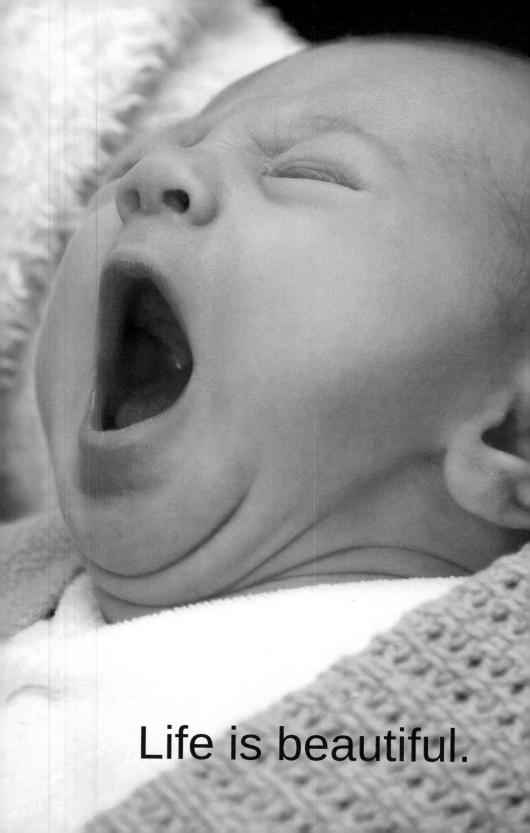

Life is beautiful.

I am proud of myself.

Everything is OK.

Life is peaceful.

I am a beautiful person.

I am loved.

Babies are magical.

I am happy.

We all love a cuddle.

All is calm.

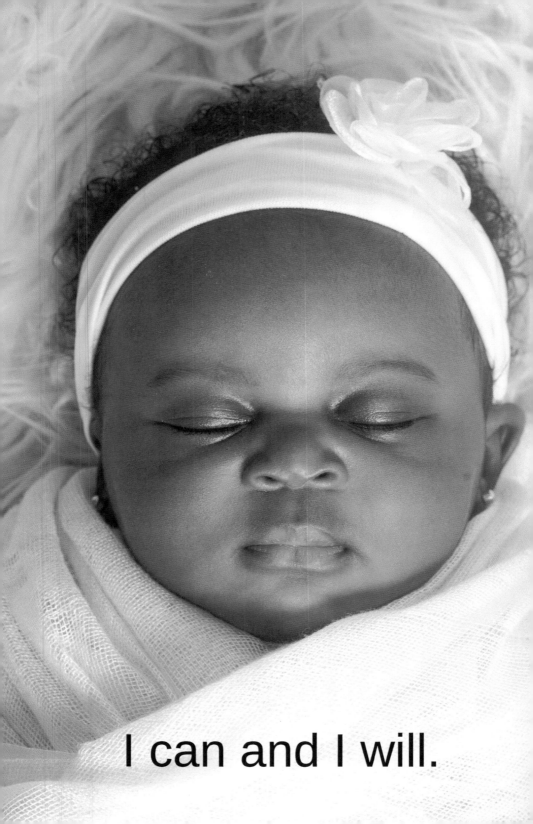

I can and I will.

Laughter is the best medicine.

Go with the flow.

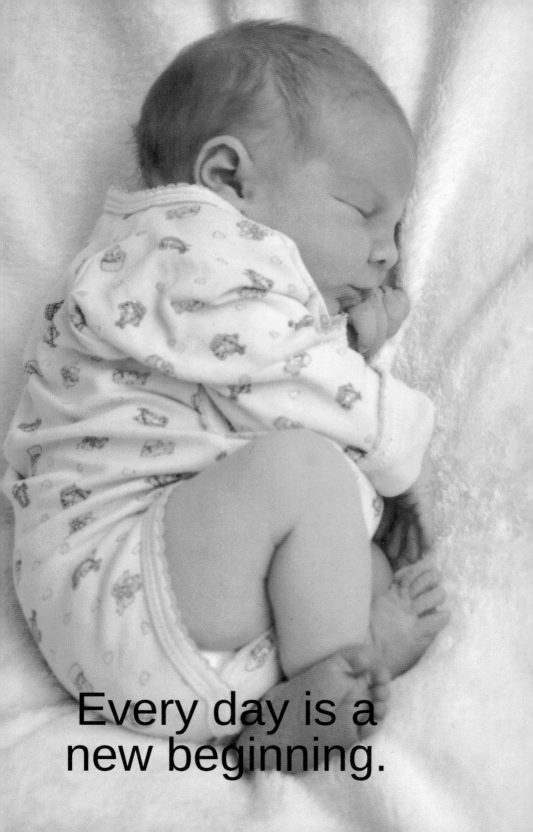

Every day is a
new beginning.

I am calm and mindful.

Life is beautiful.

There is plenty of time.

I choose happiness.

Babies are soft.

I have all that I need.

Peek-a-boo!

Babies are adorable.

I am cared for.

Babies smell delightful.

Feel a babies
soft skin.

Everything will work
out well.

I can do this.

Loved and cared for.

Beauty is all around us.

All is well.

Life is a journey.

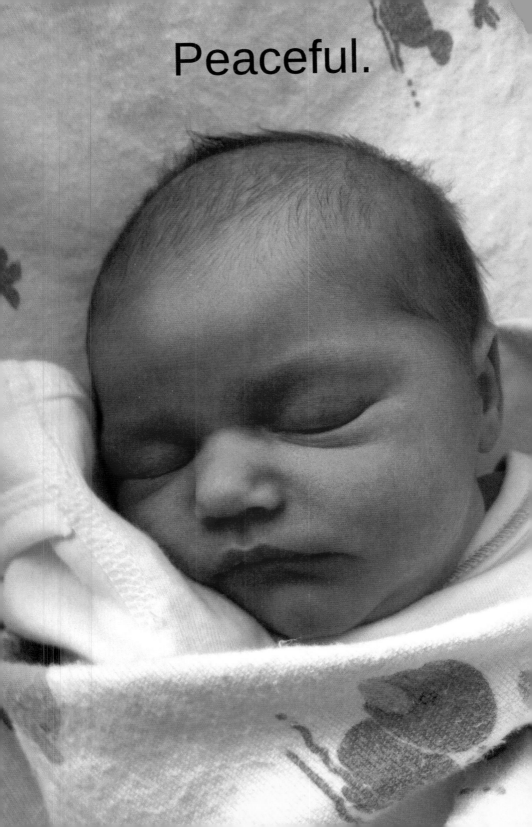

Peaceful.

I feel relaxed.

New life is beautiful.

Printed in Great Britain
by Amazon